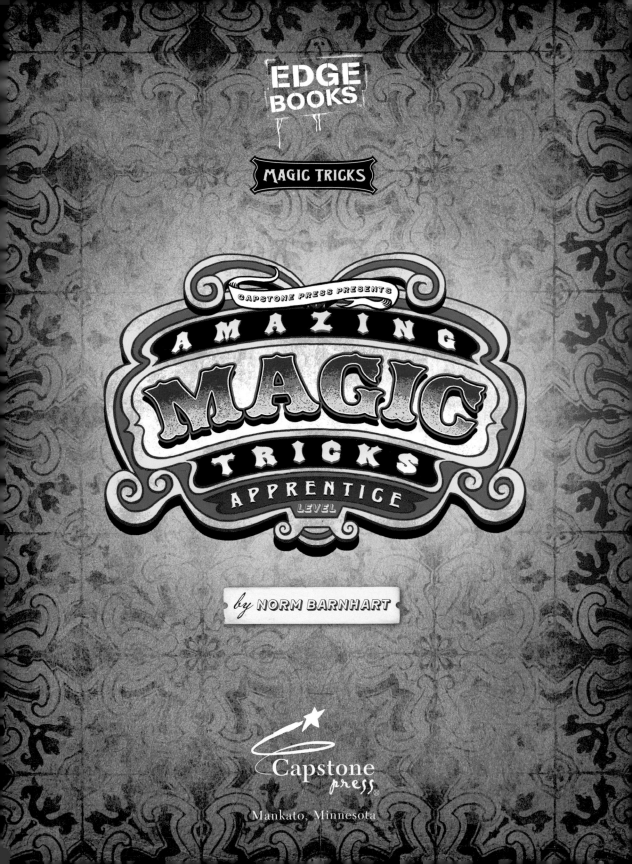

EDGE BOOKS™

MAGIC TRICKS

CAPSTONE PRESS PRESENTS

AMAZING
MAGIC
TRICKS
APPRENTICE
LEVEL

by NORM BARNHART

Capstone press®

Mankato, Minnesota

Edge Books are published by Capstone Press,
151 Good Counsel Drive, P.O. Box 669, Mankato, Minnesota 56002.
www.capstonepress.com

Library of Congress Cataloging-in-Publication Data
Barnhart, Norm.
   Amazing magic tricks: apprentice level / by Norm Barnhart.
   p. cm. — (Edge books. Magic Tricks.)
   Includes bibliographical references and index.
   Summary: "Step-by-step instructions and clear photos describe how to
perform magic tricks at the apprentice level" — Provided by publisher.
   ISBN-13: 978-1-4296-1943-1 (hardcover)
   ISBN-10: 1-4296-1943-0 (hardcover)
   1. Magic tricks — Juvenile literature. I. Title. II. Series.
GV1548.B353 2009
793.8 — dc22   2008002573

Editorial Credits
Aaron Sautter, editor; Bob Lentz, designer/illustrator; Marcy Morin, scheduler

Photo Credits
Capstone Press/Karon Dubke, cover, objects, magic steps
Shutterstock/Chen Ping Hung; javarman; Marilyn Volan;
   Tatiana53; Tischenko Irina, backgrounds

**Capstone Press thanks Anthony Wacholtz of Compass Point Books and
Hilary Wacholz of Picture Window Books for their help in producing this book.**

1 2 3 4 5 6 13 12 11 10 09 08

TABLE OF CONTENTS

BOOK 2

MYSTERIOUS MAGIC!

Magicians have performed mysterious magic tricks for hundreds of years. They have rarely shared their secrets with anyone. But by opening this book, you'll discover the secret of making things vanish or appear. And you'll astound audiences with your mysterious mental powers. Are you ready? It's time to do some magic!

THE KEYS TO MAGIC

➜ Practice, practice, practice! If you want your tricks to work right, you need to practice until you can do them quickly and smoothly. Try standing in front of a mirror while practicing. Then you can see what the tricks will look like to your audience.

➜ Keep it secret! Magicians never share their secrets. If you reveal the secrets of a trick, people won't be very impressed. It also ruins the trick for other magicians who want to do it in the future.

➜ Be entertaining! Try telling the audience some jokes or stories that relate to your tricks while performing them. Keep the audience entertained and they won't notice how the tricks are done. It will also keep them coming back for more.

ASSISTANTS

BEFORE YOU BEGIN

Most magicians hide their props in a magic box. A magic box will help you keep your tricks organized and your special props hidden from the audience. You can make your own magic box. Find a cardboard box and decorate it with some colorful stars, or cover it with dark cloth so it looks mysterious.

A magic wand is one of a magician's most useful tools. Wands help direct people's attention to what you want them to see. You can make a wand out of a wooden dowel painted black and white. Or roll up a piece of black construction paper and tape the ends. You can add sparkles and stars if you wish. Be creative and have fun!

A MAGIC SECRET - ASSISTANTS

Magicians often need assistants to help them perform their tricks. Most assistants are really secret helpers who know the secrets behind the tricks. Sometimes they sit in the crowd and pretend to be part of the audience. Assistants help the magician make the tricks look real. Find a good secret assistant, and you'll have lots of fun fooling people with your magic tricks.

THE MAGIC ROBOT

Some robots seem to have magical abilities. In this trick, the audience will gasp when they see a toy robot magically move from your pocket back to its box.

WHAT YOU NEED:

> → Two identical toy robots
> → A small box

PREPARATION:

1. First, cut a hole in the back of the box as shown. Be sure the hole is large enough to fit your finger. Then place both robots into the box.

PERFORMANCE:

2. Start by picking up the box and holding one of the toy robots with your finger as shown. Tip over the box and drop the other robot into your hand. Don't let the audience see that you're holding the secret robot inside the box.

3. Next, show the audience the robot and tell them a story about how it can perform an amazing magic act. Explain how it can move so fast that they won't even see it move. Then place the robot in your pocket.

4. Hold up the box and wave your magic wand over it. You can say some made-up magic words to help fool the audience. Or you can pretend that you feel something jump out of your pocket.

5. Finally, tip over the box and drop the hidden robot into your hand. Show it to the audience and have it take a bow!

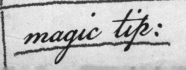

magic tip: Be sure to keep the hole in the box hidden from the audience. If they see it, they'll learn the secret of the trick.

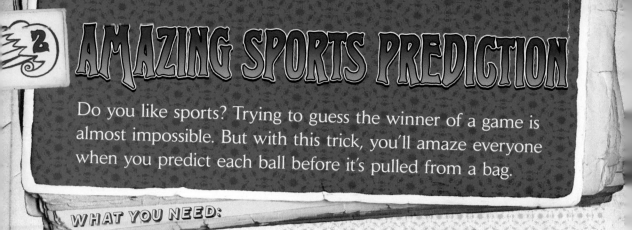

AMAZING SPORTS PREDICTION

Do you like sports? Trying to guess the winner of a game is almost impossible. But with this trick, you'll amaze everyone when you predict each ball before it's pulled from a bag.

WHAT YOU NEED:

→ Several small toy sports balls
→ A small paper bag
→ Scissors

PREPARATION:

1. First, cut a small hole in the bottom back corner of the paper bag as shown.

2. Then fold the bag back again so the hole is hidden.

3. First, tell the audience about your amazing predictions. Tell them you can guess which ball will be pulled out of the bag.

Pick up the bag and unfold it, making sure to keep the hole hidden. Pinch the hole closed so nobody sees it, then show the audience that the bag is empty.

4. Now ask a volunteer to drop the balls into the bag. Then hold the bag by the front upper corner as shown. Be sure to hold the bag so the secret hole faces you. The balls will roll to the rear. You should be able to see a bit of one ball through the secret hole. If you see the baseball say, "I predict that the baseball will be picked first."

5. Finally, close your eyes and reach into the bag. Go to the back corner, pull out the baseball, and show it to the audience. Do this twice more, announcing which ball will be picked each time. When the balls are gone, crumple up the bag and toss it in your magic box. Everyone will wonder how you made your amazing predictions!

THE PHOENIX BALLOON

Is it possible to put a popped balloon back together again? It is with this fun trick. The audience will be stunned when they see a popped balloon magically made whole again.

WHAT YOU NEED:

> Two identical balloons
> A large paper bag
> A fork

PREPARATION:

1. First, blow up one balloon and tie it. Then place it at the bottom of the paper bag as shown. Place the empty balloon in the bag so it can be dumped out easily.

PERFORMANCE:

2. Start by telling the audience about your magic balloon. Say, "This balloon can restore itself if it's popped!" Then tip over the bag so the empty balloon drops onto the table. Don't let the secret filled balloon fall out.

3. Next, blow up the empty balloon, tie it, and show it to the audience. Then pop it with the fork and place the pieces back into the bag. You can have fun by saying something like, "This looks bad. I don't know if the balloon can fix itself this time!"

4. Now close the top of the bag and wave your magic wand over it. You can say a few made-up magic words too.

5. Finally, open up the bag and pull out the filled balloon. The audience will think the balloon magically restored itself. Take a bow as they applaud!

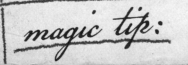

Try adding some fun to this trick. Pretend that the balloon pieces are jumping around in the bag as they try to join together again.

THE AMAZING BRAIN-E-O

Use the power of your brain to read people's minds! Your friends will be amazed as you tell them what objects they are thinking about. It's easy when you know the secret.

WHAT YOU NEED:

→ Ten random objects
→ A secret assistant

PERFORMANCE:

1. Start this trick by telling the audience about your amazing mind-reading powers. Tell them you can read their minds and that you can prove it. Ask your secret assistant to help with this trick. Then turn your back to the audience.

2. While your back is turned, your assistant asks a volunteer to choose an object on the table. The volunteer should not say the object's name out loud. Instead, the volunteer should just point at the chosen object.

3. Before doing this trick, you should arrange to have your assistant point at the chosen object on the third try. Now turn back to the table. Your assistant should point to a different object and ask if it is the chosen item. You'll say, "No, that's not correct."

4. Your assistant then points at a second item on the table. Concentrate hard on that object and act as if you aren't sure if it's correct. Finally, you'll say, "No that's not the right one either."

5. On the third try, your assistant will point at the correct object. Now act like the trick has become really easy and say, "Yes, that's it!" The audience will be stunned by your amazing mind-reading powers!

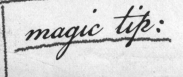

magic tip: Try this trick again, but this time the chosen item will be the fifth one your assistant points to. The audience will wonder how you can read their minds!

THE PUZZLING PUZZLE

You can use your mind powers to do more than just guess what people are thinking. You will really leave your audience puzzled with this mind-bending puzzle trick!

WHAT YOU NEED:

→ Two small, identical puzzles
→ Two small paper bags
→ Scissors
→ Tape

1

PREPARATION:

1. First, cut one bag in half lengthwise as shown. Be sure to leave the bottom of the bag attached.

magic tip: Use some glue or tape on the back of the hidden puzzle to hold it together while it's inside the secret pocket.

2. Then place the cut bag inside the whole bag. Tape the sides to hold it in place. This creates a secret pocket on one side where you can hide a puzzle.

3. Next, assemble one of the puzzles, but leave one piece out. Then slide the puzzle into the secret pocket as shown.

PERFORMANCE:

4. First, tell the audience about your mysterious mind powers. Say, "Puzzles are fun, but they take too long to put together. I like using my mind instead." Then tip the bag over to show the audience that it's empty. As you tip it, hold the secret pocket closed as shown.

TURN PAGE FOR MORE!

5. Next, drop the puzzle pieces into the bag. Leave one puzzle piece on the table. This piece should match the one you left out before. You can mark the back of it to remember which piece it is.

6. Now shake the bag gently. Pretend that you're concentrating hard to put the puzzle together with the power of your mind.

7. Slowly pull the hidden puzzle out of the secret pocket. Be sure the audience can see that the puzzle is fully assembled, except for one missing piece. Then toss the bag into your magic box.

8. Finally, pick up the extra puzzle piece and place it into the puzzle. Leaving one piece out helps the audience believe that you really assembled the puzzle with your mind. Take a bow while the audience applauds your mysterious mind powers!

IT'S PARTY TIME!

Celebrate the New Year, a friend's birthday, or any special occasion with this fun, flashy trick. You'll be the life of the party when you make a shower of confetti instantly appear.

WHAT YOU NEED:

→ Two identical file folders
→ A sheet of colorful paper
→ A marker
→ Scissors
→ Glue

PREPARATION:

1. First, cut 1 inch (2.5 centimeters) off the top of one folder. Then glue one side of the short folder inside the other folder as shown.

2. Next, cut the sheet of paper in half. Using the marker, write a message like "Happy New Year!" on both halves of the paper. Then cut one half of the paper into confetti. Place it in one of the open sections inside the folder as shown.

3. Tell the audience, "It's time for a party!" Then show them the empty section of the folder.

Next, show the audience the uncut paper with the message written on it. Then place it into the empty section of the folder.

4. Now it's time for the magic. Concentrate hard on the folder and say a few magic words. Pretend that you're cutting up the paper inside with magic invisible scissors as shown.

5. Finally, pop open the folder so a shower of confetti fills the air! Be sure to keep the uncut paper hidden inside the closed section of the folder. Put the folder in your magic box and take a bow!

magic tip: Make sure none of the confetti falls out when you show the empty folder to the audience. If they see it, they'll know you cheated!

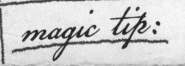

THE FREAKY MIND WELD

Paper clips are easy to lose. It's easier to keep track of them if they're linked together. This trick will astonished your audience when they see your magic mind powers at work!

WHAT YOU NEED:

> → 20 paper clips
> → An envelope
> → Glue

PREPARATION:

1. First, link ten paper clips and place them in the corner of the envelope. Next, glue the inside of the envelope as shown to make a secret pocket. The linked clips will be sealed inside. Then put the ten loose clips into the open part of the envelope.

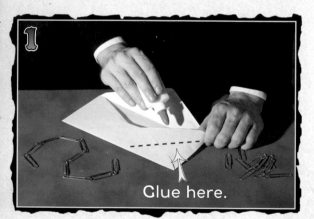

1

Glue here.

PERFORMANCE:

2. Show the envelope to the audience and say, "I found an easy way to keep paper clips together." Open the envelope and pour out the loose clips.

2

3. Tell the audience, "All I have to do is link the clips together with my mind." Put the clips back in the envelope, one at a time. Count out loud as you do this so the audience knows how many paper clips there are. Then lick the envelope and seal it.

4. Now hold the envelope up to your forehead. Pretend to use your powerful mental energy to link the paper clips together. Pretending to concentrate hard makes this trick seem really mysterious for the audience.

5. Now rip open the end of the envelope with the secret pocket. Grab the end of the linked clips and slowly pull them out. The audience will be astonished when they see that the clips are linked together. You have one powerful brain!

magic tip: Try attaching a small toy soldier to the end of the paper clip chain. Then pretend to be surprised when you find that the soldier did all the work!

MESSAGE FROM A GHOST

You can freak out your friends with this spooky trick. When your pet ghost sends you a creepy message, they'll be too scared to move!

WHAT YOU NEED:

- → A shoebox
- → Two sheets of paper
- → A marker

PREPARATION:

1. Write a creepy message like "Boo!" on one sheet of paper. Crumple the message into a ball. Then place it into the shoebox with the blank sheet of paper. Keep the marker and cover of the shoebox in your magic box.

PERFORMANCE:

2. Tell your friends you have a pet ghost and that it likes to leave you messages. Get out the shoebox and take out the blank sheet of paper. At the same time, secretly hide the crumpled ball in your hand as shown.

Message

Message

Blank paper

3. Show that the paper is blank on both sides, then crumple it into a ball. As you crumple it, secretly switch it with the paper hidden in your hand. Then drop the message into the shoebox. Be sure to keep the blank paper hidden in your hand.

4. Next, get the marker and shoebox cover out of your magic box. When you reach in, drop the blank paper. Toss the marker into the shoebox and put on the cover. Then shake the box and pretend to wrestle with it as if your pet ghost was moving around inside.

5. Finally, remove the shoebox cover and take out the paper. Ask someone to open it and read it. Your friends will be amazed at the spooky message that has appeared!

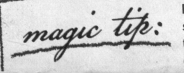

magic tip: Before doing this trick, try telling the audience a story about the ghost. Maybe you trapped it by the light of the full moon. Or maybe it's a friendly ghost that likes to help out with your magic show!

WHERE'S ROVER?

Mental magic can help you read people's minds, make predictions, or put a puzzle together. And with this astounding trick, it can even help you find a lost dog!

WHAT YOU NEED:

→ Three cups
→ A small toy dog
→ A secret assistant
→ A table

PERFORMANCE:

1. First, show the toy dog and the cups to the audience, then set the props on the table. Tell the audience you have a special mental connection with the dog. Say, "Rover is my special pal. I can find him even if he gets lost under the cups."

2. Next, ask your secret assistant, who is sitting in the audience, to come and help you with this trick. Then turn your back to the table. Ask your secret assistant to place the toy dog under one of the cups and mix them up.

3. Turn back to the table when your assistant is done. Then begin pretending to use your mental powers to see which cup the dog is under.

You will be able to find the correct cup by looking at your secret assistant's feet.

4. If the dog is under the left cup, your assistant's foot will point to the left.

If the dog is under the center cup, your assistant's feet both point forward.

If the dog is under the right cup, your assistant's foot will point to the right.

5. Once you know where the toy dog is, lift up the cup to reveal the toy. The audience will be stunned by your awesome mental powers!

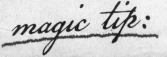

magic tip: Be sure to practice this trick with your secret assistant before performing it. If he or she acts cool and calm, everything should go smoothly.

RICKY, THE WONDER RABBIT

Magicians love using rabbits in their acts. But some rabbits are fun tricksters themselves! You can astonish your friends with this card trick using a tricky stuffed bunny.

WHAT YOU NEED:

→ A deck of cards
→ A stuffed toy rabbit

PREPARATION:

1. Place all the red cards on the bottom of the deck and all the black cards on the top. When fanned out, the black cards and red cards should be grouped together as shown.

PERFORMANCE:

2. Start by introducing Ricky the Wonder Rabbit to your audience. Say, "Ricky can find a secret hidden card with his amazing sense of smell!"

3. Next, fan out the top half of the deck as shown. Make sure that only the black cards are fanned out. Then ask a volunteer to choose a card and show it to the audience, but not to you or Ricky the Rabbit. This should be one of the black cards.

4. While the volunteer shows the card to the audience, fan the deck as shown so only the red cards are fanned out. Then ask the volunteer to slide the chosen card back into the fanned part of the deck.

5. Now the black card should be mixed in with the red cards and very easy to find. This is the secret of the trick.

TURN PAGE FOR MORE!

6. Now fan out the deck so only you can see the cards. Take the chosen black card from the deck and lay it face down on the table. Tell the volunteer, "I'm not sure, but I think your card could be this one." Be sure to remember where this card is on the table.

7. Take five more cards and lay them on the table in the same way. There will be a total of six cards on the table. Each time you pick a card, tell the volunteer you think it could be the chosen card, but you aren't sure. Be sure to remember where the correct card is.

magic tip: You can make this trick really fun by pretending to scold Ricky for fooling you with his trickery!

8. Now it's time for Ricky the Wonder Rabbit to do his famous trick. Have some fun by handling the rabbit like a puppet. Have Ricky sniff a card. He'll shake his head "no." Flip over the card to show it's not the volunteer's chosen card.

9. Keep playing with Ricky like he's real. Have Ricky sniff at each card and shake his head "no" until there are just two cards left. Make sure one of the leftover cards is the correct one.

10. Now say, "Okay Ricky, there are only two cards left. This is your last chance." Have Ricky sniff at the correct card. Ricky should go wild – bouncing and jumping around. Finally, he'll land on the correct card. Flip over the chosen card and show it to the audience. Have Ricky take a bow as they applaud!

GLOSSARY

astound (uh-STOUND) — to amaze or astonish

audience (AW-dee-uhnss) — people who watch or listen to a play, movie, or show

concentrate (KAHN-suhn-trayt) — to focus your thoughts and attention on something

confetti (kuhn-FET-ee) — small pieces of colored paper that people throw at parties, parades, and other celebrations

dowel (DOUL) — a round wooden rod

mental power (MEN-tuhl POU-ur) — the ability to do something with the mind, such as finding hidden objects or reading others' thoughts

predict (pri-DIKT) — to say what you think will happen in the future

prop (PROP) — an item used by an actor or performer during a show

volunteer (vol-uhn-TIHR) — someone who offers to help perform a task during a show

READ MORE

Longe, Bob. *Easy Card Magic*. New York: Sterling, 2003.

Mandelberg, Robert. *Easy Mind-Reading Tricks*. New York: Sterling, 2005.

Zenon, Paul. *Gimmicks and Card Tricks: Illusions for the Intermediate Magician*. Amazing Magic. New York: Rosen, 2008.

INTERNET SITES

FactHound offers a safe, fun way to find Internet sites related to this book. All of the sites on FactHound have been researched by our staff.

Here's how:
1. Visit *www.facthound.com*
2. Choose your grade level.
3. Type in this book ID **1429619430** for age-appropriate sites. You may also browse subjects by clicking on letters, or by clicking on pictures and words.
4. Click on the **Fetch It** button.

FactHound will fetch the best sites for you!

About the author

Norm Barnhart is a professional comic magician who has entertained audiences for more than 28 years. In 2007, Norm was named America's Funniest Magician by the Family Entertainers Workshop. Norm's travels have taken him across the United States and to five other countries. He also loves getting kids excited about reading. Norm says, "I love bringing smiles to people's faces with magic. After reading this book, kids will love doing magic too."